WEIRD, WILD & WONDERFUL

For every school that's invited me in; for every teacher
that's made me welcome; for all the children that have
read me their fabulous poems... JC

For the poets who enrich our lives NL

Love You More is for Sarah
She's... and *Conversation with a Fly* are for Sarah, Lauren and Madeleine
The Cat is for Alice
She Watches the World and *Who Cares* were written for National Poetry
Day
This Is Where... is for South Moreton Primary School
School Library! and *How Easily* are for Falkland Primary School, Newbury

Very special thanks to JW, BM and the one and only GTD.
And of course, big thanks to illustrator extraordinaire, Neal Layton –
for bringing his brilliance to the world of our book.

*She Watches the World, The Elephant's Ode to the Dung Beetle, Who Cares?,
River, Have You Ever, It's... Kindness, That's Poetry* and *How Easily* are
first published in 2021 in *Weird, Wild and Wonderful*. All other poems
have been selected from previous James Carter collections: *Cars Stars
Electric Guitars, Time-Travelling Underpants, Hey, Little Bug! Greetings
Earthlings!, Journey to the Centre of My Brain, GRRR!, I'm a Little Alien!,
The World's Greatest Space Cadet, Spooky Poems* and *Spaced Out*.

Weird, Wild and Wonderful text copyright © James Carter 2021
Illustrations copyright © Neal Layton 2021
First published in Great Britain and in the USA in 2021 by
Otter-Barry Books, Little Orchard, Burley Gate, Herefordshire, HR1 3QS
www.otterbarrybooks.com

A catalogue record for this book is available from the British Library.

Designed by Arianna Osti

ISBN 978-1-91307-473-9

Illustrated with pencil, pen and ink with digital media

Set in New Century School Book

Printed in Great Britain

9 8 7 6 5 4 3 2 1

WEIRD, WILD & WONDERFUL

THE POETRY WORLD OF JAMES CARTER

Illustrated by NEAL LAYTON

Otter-Barry BOOKS

CoNTEnTs

WiLD

nature poems, beastly poems

WoNDeRFUL

science poems, quiet poems

A Few Words from James Carter

There's a Magic Wood at the back of my house.
If ever I'm seeking inspiration, I'll take off at night
to wander through the wood, through the shadows,
throughs the beams of a midnight moon until I find the
Magic Tree. Hidden in its twisted roots is a tiny magic
book entitled *1001 Magic Ideas For...* Hang on – you
don't believe a word of this, do you? Fair enough. But
we've all got our own Magic Wood. You most likely call
it your *imagination*.

Like all writers, I'm curious. I'm fascinated by this
old planet we inhabit – from the world around me to
the wide world at large. In the poem *The Big Things* –
that's me up in that tree wondering what it's all about,
while my neighbour is thinking 'What's he going on
about *now*?' And beyond curiosity, I write because
I absolutely love words.

This book has poems that feature things I've seen,
read about, thought about, experienced or observed
– and my Magic Wood, sorry – *imagination* – simply
takes them, ponders over them, and then weaves
words around them as I try to find brand-new ways
of showing these things back to the world. I'm saying,
'Hey, look at that – but look at it like this...'

Most poems come about from something happening in my life – *Tree* happened after I felt guilty about having a tree in our garden chopped down. I wrote *She's...* for Mothers' Day. *How Easily* was a leavers' poem for a Year 6 class.

The poems in this book are mainly those that people have seemed to connect with, and there are also a few new ones – plus a couple of my personal favourites too. They began at home, or on trains, or on walks, on hilltops, in real woods, in cafés – all over the place. But if I hadn't had the life-changingly fabulous experience of being a dad to my two daughters, this would pretty much be an empty book. For they showed me the world afresh.

So welcome to my *Weird, Wild and Wonderful* world, or maybe Magic Wood...

James Carter

WEIRD

daft poems, cheeky poems

What Did You Do at School Today?

Nothing.

Nothing?

Well, nothing much.

You did nothing much all day long?

Well... all right Mum, if you really want to know,
I had 4 lessons
and 45 minutes of playtime
in which I went around with 3 friends.
For lunch I ate 22 baked beans,
2 fishfingers and a bit of a banana.
I fed Nibbles, the class hamster,
1 sunflower seed.
I wrote 1 poem.
I got 7/10 for a spelling test.
I did 16 fairly tricky maths questions.

And... I learnt 5 very interesting things
about the Ancient Egyptians, including
how they used to remove the brains
of their dead with a – MUM...
DO YOU EVER LISTEN TO A SINGLE
WORD I SAY?

Oh sorry, darling – what was that?

I said I removed my teacher's brain today!

What? Oh well done, you –
what would you like for tea?

What Will I Be
When I Grow Up?

Mum says: 'Happy.'

Dad says: 'Older – and taller.'

My aunty says: 'Anything you want to be.'

My uncle says: 'An adult!'

My teacher says: 'Wiser.'

And Gran says: 'Brilliant.'

And I say: *How on earth do they know?*

What Makes Me Me?

I've been told I've got –

Mum's ears
Dad's hair
Gran's chin
and
Aunty Emma's sense of humour…

**will they ever
want them back,
d'you think?**

The Really Really Really Truly True Truth about...Teddy Bears

Everybody has a teddy.
Even if they say they don't, they do,
they're fibbing. Even kings, queens,

famous footballers, hairy rock stars
and busy teachers. Yours included.
And all those people on the telly. Them too.

And I'm sure even aliens have their own
equally cute, equally cuddly, equally
dog-eared, squished and dribbled-over

version of this classic soft toy. But why?
Well, why not? However old you are,
however grown up you may appear to be,

however important or bossy you become,
in a hush of a moment every now and then,
you will still feel the need to open

the bedroom cupboard, remove
that little fuzzy bundle, and give it
a sniff and a kiss and a little snuggle.

Lullaby for a Woolly Mammoth

(to the tune of Twinkle, Twinkle…)

Woolly
Mammoth!
Hear me sing.
! Go to sleep you hairy thing!
! You   can snooze outside my
! door   just as long as you don't
!   !   snore. Come on Shaggy, shut
  !   your eyes.   Now it's
                    time for   beddy-byes!

Electric Guitars

I like electric guitars:
played mellow or moody
frantic or fast – on CDs
or tapes, at home or in
cars – live in the streets
at gigs or in bars.
I like
electric
guitars:
played
choppy
like
reggae
or angry
like
rock or
chirpy
like
jazz or
strummy
like
pop or
heavy
like
metal – it
bothers
me not.
I like electric guitars:
their strings and their straps
and their wild wammy bars – their
jangling and twanging and funky
wah-wahs – their fuzz boxes,
frets and multi-effects –
pick-ups, machine
heads, mahogany necks –
their plectrums, their wires,
and big amplifiers. I like electric
guitars: played loudly, politely – dully
or brightly – daily or nightly – badly
or nicely. I like electric guitars:
bass, lead and rhythm –
I basically dig 'em –
I like electric
guitars

Learn How to Play Air Guitar

in under 20 seconds – or your money back!

**Just follow these Seven Simple Steps
to Air Guitar Heaven:**

I. **MAKE SURE YOUR AIR GUITAR IS IN TUNE**:
pretend to fiddle with the imaginary tuning pegs
and make some strange tuning sounds with your
mouth.

2. **DON'T JUST STRUM IT MADLY**: make it *look
like* you know what you're doing. Play a mean and
moody rock riff. And why not take a solo? And don't
forget to use the old wammy bar.

3. **IF YOU HAVEN'T GOT EXTREMELY LONG
HAIR, FAKE IT BABY**: pretend you've got hair
that hangs all the way down your back. Now swish it
from side to side and backwards and forwards as you
are playing. Yeahhhhhh!

4. **GET SOME NIFTY POSES GOING ON**: try the
'windmill' strum or the leg-in-the-air 'duck walk'.
Get down on your knees and sway wildly from side
to side. If in doubt, just make stuff up.

5. PULL SOME REALLY WEIRD FACES:
practise in the mirror first, you don't want to look
too weird. You could try closing your eyes and a)
pretending your teeth are glued together, or b) better
still, pretending your tongue is glued to your chin.
Coooool!

6. CHECK NO ONE IS LOOKING: then check
again. And again. Turn the music up and get. . .

7. *ROCKIN'!!!!*

Conversation with a Fly

ZZZZ!

Oh, hello, fly!

ZZZZ!

What are you up to, then?

ZZZZ!

Sorry, I didn't catch that…

ZZZZ!

No, I still didn't get it.

ZZZZ!

Are you trying to tell me something?

ZZZZ!

Something important, perhaps?

ZZZZ!

Is something the matter, maybe?

ZZZZ!

Are you in some kind of trouble?

ZZZZ!

Look. I don't understand 'zzzz!'

ZZZZ!

Please don't keep saying 'zzzz!'

ZZZZ!

Right, fly. I'll give you one more chance, okay?

zzzzzzzzZZZ!!!

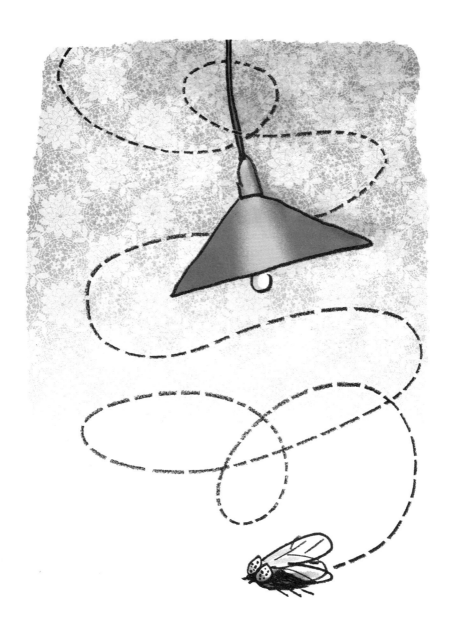

The BIG Things

Early evening
I'm sitting in my favourite tree
gazing at the moon
in the pale summer sky
just thinking

Thinking about the big things:
like time
and infinity
and the cosmos

and how
our little misty marble
of a planet
keeps spinning around
in that great murky soup
we call space

When Keith – my next-door neighbour –
peers over the fence
and says, 'What you doin'
up there then?'

And I say,
'Well, Keith –
I was thinking…

about the unstoppableness of time
and the smallness of me
and the whopping great bigness of space
and things.'

And Keith says, 'Oh, right.'

And I jump down
from the tree
climb over the fence
and say, 'Keith?
Do you ever
think about time
and space and life
and what it
all means and stuff?' And Keith says,
'Fancy a game of footie?'

And I say, 'Do you, Keith?
And do you think about
how the planets all turn together
like the cogs of a massive cosmic clock?'

And Keith says,
'Look, you playing footie or what?'

And I say,
'No seriously, Keith,
do you think about it?'

And Keith says,
'I'll go in goal.'

And I say,
'Oh... *whatever.*'

What Can You Do with a Football?

*Well... you can **kick it** you can **catch it** you can **bounce it** all around. You can **grab it** you can **pat it** you can **roll it** on the ground. You can **throw it** you can **head it** you can **hit it** – with a bat. You can **biff it** you can **boot it** you can **spin it** you can **shoot it**. You can **drop it** you can **stop it** – just like that!*

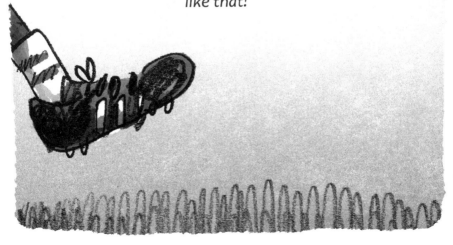

```
          vvvvvvv
       vvvvvvvvvvvvv
     vvvvvvvvvvvvvvvvv
   vvvvvvvvvvvvvvvvvvvvv
  @          vvvv          @
  @   +++    vvvv    +++   @
  @    v     vvvv     v    @
  @          vvvv          @
  @           v            @
  @                        @
     @     WE'RE...   @
       @            @
           @@@
```
Dark Agers.
Land invaders. Craft
traders. Ocean gravers. Myth-
!! makers. Longboat sailors. Wave !!
!!   riders. Fierce fighters. Great   !!
!!   survivors. Kenning scribers.   !!
!!   Nordic dwellers. Beardy   !!
!!   fellas. Bling pinchers?   !!
!!   Well, yes - we're THE   !!
!!!!   **VIKINGS!** Did you   !!!!
           guess??
          ??   ??
          ??   ??
          ??   ??
          ??   ??
          ??   ??
          ??   ??
         ????   ????

28

Spot the Fairy Tales

(Ten Tiny Senryū)

Enter if you dare –
three breakfasts; one broken chair.
Off to bed? ***Bewar**e…*

A cute bird calling
an urgent word of warning –
'THE SKY IS FALLING!!'

What a bossy titch –
told us not to cross his bridge.
This grass is *de-lish*…

So no porky pies:
but plenty huffs and puffs…plus
a hot bot to boot!

'Here's my cunning plan:
If I can't nab young Hoodie,
I'll go grab her Gran!'

'Hey babe, way up there –
I've found neither lift nor stair –
please let down your hair!'

Since that evil spell
he's felt *Beast*ly, none too well.
Hey, who rings that *Belle*?

Princess – what to do?
Ignore that *warty one*, or...
try a kissie-poo?

Seems like royalty.
Picky eater? Light sleeper –
when upon a pea...

She's poshed up in bling –
grooving with the future king.
Slipper fits. ***KERCHING!***

31

The Wonderful World
of Weird!

In the World of Weird
all the girls wear beards
and the boys keep bees in their beds
the girls dig holes and live like moles
and the boys grow trees on their heads

In the World of Weird
all the oranges are blue
and the lemons are as sweet as can be
bananas are round and they grow in the ground
or down at the bottom of the sea

In the World of Weird
all the fish can fly
and the chips are fried in lakes
the dogs love cats: with sauce, of course
served up on silver plates

Now how do you get
to the World of Weird?
Where is it? Where is it? Where?
Hop on a bee – pop over the sea
then give us a call when you're there!

33

WiLD

nature poems, beastly poems

Wild!

Wild the garden overgrown
wild the jaw that breaks the bone

Wild the rain that soaks the sand
wild the sun that cracks the land

Wild the summer's green and greed
wild the wind that sows the seed

Wild the flower, big in bloom
wild the early dawning tune

Wild the bird that seeks the sun
wild the cry when life is done

Wild the claw that rips the skin
wild the bite, the tear, the sting

Wild the young that feed to grow
wild the blood that stains the snow

Wild the stench of fresh decay
wild the mulch that rots away

Wild the winter's yearly cull
wild the springtime's early bulb

Wild the thorn, the fruit, the bud
wild the roots, the shoots, the mud

Wild the song, the forest hum
wild the rhythm in the drum

Wild the honey in the comb
wild the hunter heading home

Wild the worm that breaks the soil
wild the world in constant toil

Wild the weed that lives in cracks
wild the scythe, the saw, the axe

Wild the heart at trees laid bare
wild that wild no longer there

The Wolf Outside

I wake.   I know.
No need   to see.
A visitor has come for me. That
wolf is at the door again. In the
dark, the pouring rain. He makes
no sound – he needs to hear my
breath, my pulse, my thoughts,
my fear. We wait together. Two
souls still. I need to live, he
needs to kill. He leaves – I
breathe. I sigh and how.
I check. The wolf
has gone …
for now.

Between the Dog and the Wolf

(after Aesop)

A wolf once chanced upon a dog
beyond the wild wood.
Cried Wolf, 'And how are you today?'
Barked Dog, 'Well, life is good:

I'm loved, I'm fed, and warm's my bed.
So me, I'm doing fine.'
'Fed?' cried Wolf, and, 'Warm?' he said.
'I'd swap your life for mine.'

'I'm starved,' moaned Wolf, 'I'm cold. Afraid.
My life is constant strain.
And every day I struggle on
through wind, through snow, through rain.'

'But what,' asked Wolf, 'is that old thing?'
'Oh that,' laughed Dog, 'it's great –
my collar's how they tie me up
so I will not escape.

And that's not all, it bears my name.
I run when I am called.
Or fetch a stick, or do a trick.
A dog is not ignored!'

'A name?' cried Wolf. 'Have you no shame?
A beast must keep its soul.
You're better dead than tame,' he said.
'You have been truly sold…

…however hard my life may get
my spirit must be free.
I'll keep my moon, my stars, my dark,
my space to live and be.'

With this, the wolf began to cry
a tortured, whining growl –
so horrified by brother Dog:
that's how it learnt to howl.

She watches the world

through star-gold eyes:

with awe but mostly
suspicion; she'll sniff

at the air, she'll wait,
she'll listen, she'll sense

the slightest footfall;
she'll skulk through the night

in her old winter coat
beneath an ocean of sky;

she'll leap over snow
with limbs as fleet

as the wind's invisible wings;
she'll follow the promise

of even the wisp
of a meal.

Here in my dreams,
those darkest woods,

nothing bewitches me
more than her:

that great grey wolf.

Elephant

Where on earth
would you begin
to paint an elephant?

That quick-witted,
ocean-memoried,
grey hunk of a thing?

Linking
tail-to-trunk
tail-to-trunk
over the
dusty plains?

Marching through
the clatter
of some summer
street parade?

Or alone
out there
in the starry dark,
turning the bones
of one long gone?

And what would
you paint it with?

Colours
or words?

The Elephant's ODE to the DUNG BEETLE

Dung dung dung

Dung dung dung

Dung dung dung

Dung dung dung

Dung dung dung

Dung dung dung

Oh, Beetle,
you're a star, you
are – you brighten up my
day, for if I ever do a dung
you roll the thing away – that's
over hills and backwards too –
and OMG – how skilled are you?
Though some may say you're
rather rude – to steal another's
poo for food. Well I say blah.
How wrong they are...
for you're a cool
recycling
dude
!

Sweet Meadow

The shortcut
to the sweet shop
was a meadow wild
with summer flowers.

Those afternoons
were hazy-hot,
that high sun
amber-bright,
and so we'd slowly
walk the mile
to the shop.

Heading home
with paper bags,
we'd stop and swap
our white mice
our pink prawns
our multi-coloured
chocolate drops:
then sugar-fingered
sit amongst the grass
and scoff the lot.

That meadow
is a road now; cars
swiftly pass today,
the grass verges
neatly cut, a dandelion
clock remains:

half blown away.

Who cares
if **we poison** the land,
the seas? **We fell** all the forests,
we topple the trees? There's plenty
more galaxies, planets like these - with
water, with air, with warmth, with light:
homes like ours just right for life. **Who cares**
if **we lose** those buzzy old bees? **Who cares**
if there's **plastic clogging** the seas? When
our blue world is **finally done,** we'll leave
this rock and mother sun, we'll zoom
on up - to way out where - there's
many more earths....
or are there?

A tree
is not like you and
me – it waits around quite
patiently – catching kites and
dropping leaves – reaching out to touch
the breeze...A tree all day will stand and stare,
clothed in summer, winter: bare – it has no shame
or modesty...Perhaps its generosity is the greatest in
the world – it gives a home to every bird, every squirrel,
feeds them too – to every dog it is a loo...And after dark
what does it do? Catch a falling star or two? Shimmy
in the old moonlight? Or maybe have a conker fight?
A tree can give an awful lot: the wood to make a
baby's cot – pencils, paper, tables, chairs – lolly
sticks as well as stairs...Without a tree we
could not live – a tree, it seems just
loves to give –
but us:
we
chop
we
take
we
burn
that's
what we
do in return

Gorilla Gazing

(London Zoo – Easter 2008)

He sits and he stares
with those old brown eyes
beyond the glass
beyond my gaze
to a time
and a place
he's never known
yet somehow
seems to remember

Where the wind
shakes the trees
where the rain
wets the leaves
where there are
no walls at all

He sits and he stares
like an ancient sage
beyond the glass
beyond my gaze
to a world
long gone
and wonders why
we're all
so far
from home

Sid

You've never met a cat
quite like Sid. He's a brute.
He's a bruiser. He's a bully, he is,
that cat from two doors down.

Sid Vicious I call him.
You should see the way
he terrifies and torments
our kittens. He's fearless.
He'd take the kill from an eagle,
the carrion from a crow.

When he walks, he doesn't slink
as much as plod and stomp.
He breathes heavy. He snarls. He scowls.

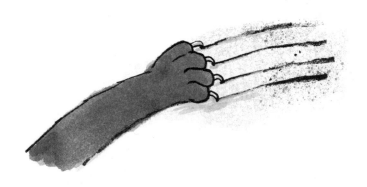

And don't you be fooled by
those delicate whiskers, those
pretty white mittens. Check out
those eyes. Deeper
than an old well. Greener
than a witch's brew.
And that coat, blacker
than the night when
the stars were stolen.

He'd pick on anyone, Sid,
anything, any size.

However tough your cat is,
don't let it out tonight.

Sid wins *every* fight.

The Cat

During the weekdays, the house
was quiet: empty of humans. The cat
had long tired of passing the time
with sleeping, moth-catching
and wall-staring and had recently taken to reading.
Luckily, the house was full of books.

There were books in every room. Best of all,
the cat enjoyed the books with poems.
Some poems, she observed, featured cats.
This pleased her greatly. Some of these cat poems,
she noticed, were good. Some very good.

Yet none, for her, expressed what it truly
feels like to be a cat. How it feels to be feline
and female. How it feels to be prodded
and poked by toddlers. How it feels
to be disrespected and distressed
by foxes and dogs. How it feels to be utterly terrified
by thunder and fireworks – and worst of all,
how it feels to have to live nine long lives.

So the cat, over time, had taken to composing
her own verse, mainly short poems that she felt
spoke of her inner self: her true catness.

Her best poem (she believed) was the soul-searching
Grey Moon In My Green Eyes, but she was also
secretly thrilled with the more upbeat kitty ditty,
Paws For Thought. However, and maddeningly,
this all led to greater frustration. For, having
created her own poetry, she had no way
of writing the verses down. Reading,
as you may know, comes quite naturally to a cat.

But writing? With a paddy paw? Like a human drawing
with oven gloves on! The best she could achieve
was to spell out a few letters on the kitchen floor
with her Catkin Crunchies. But there were never
enough Catkin Crunchies! Even a full bowl would barely
spell the poem's title out! And all her efforts would
inevitably be scooped up by a hapless human and be
returned to her bowl.

RATS! she thought. *Do all poets have to suffer like this?*

Icy Morning Haiku

On a frozen pond
a little white dog is now
attempting to skate

Way up in the tree
a black cat grins with delight
watching and waiting

Beneath the clear ice
a big fish wonders if all
dogs walk on water

From
   here
      at
        the top
     of
       the high
          green
        hill,
     with
   the
      bright
         gold
       sun
        on
         your
            fine
         brown
      back,
   today –
      right
        here
     right
      now
        old
          river,
       you
         look
           like a
        mighty
      silver
       slither;
        a shape-
       shifter
         time-
         twister
        lost in
        motion –
      cloud-borne
       rain-blessed
       soon-to-be-ocean
    so nearly free as
   the great grey waves of
THE SEA THE SEA THE SEA THE SEA THE SEA THE SEA THE
SEA THE SEA THE SEA THE SEA THE SEA THE SEA THE
SEA THE SEA THE SEA THE SEA THE SEA THE SEA

THE SEA THE SEA THE SEA THE SEA THE SEA THE SEA THE
THE SEA THE SEA THE SEA THE SEA THE SEA THE
E SEA THE SEA THE SEA THE SEA THE SEA

Tear
d
r
o
p

A

poem

is like a

tear: a drop

of emotion – a tiny

explosion – a silent

commotion – an

act of de-

votion

Have you ever

held any amber? A solid block of honey,
clear and gold, old as time? If you're lucky,
you will find there's a bug stuck inside –
when that thick 'n sticky syrup would
have oozed then dried. And it's all we'll
ever see of that sky-scraper, forest-maker
ghost of a tree. Like a poem, built to last:
it's a gift from the past, in your hand
a small reminder, yellow wonder,
precious chunk of ancient amber.

What Are Dinos Made Of?

Grr! Grr!Grr!
Grr!Grr!Grr!
Grr!
Grr!Grr!
Grr!
Grr!
Grr!   Grr!   Grr!
Grr!Grr!Grr!Grr!
Grr!   Grr!   Grr!
Grr!Grr!
Grr!Grr!Grr!
Grr!Grr!Grr!Grr!
Grr!Grr!Grr!Grr!Grr!   Grr!
Grr!Grr!Grr!Grr! Grr!   Grr!
Grr!   Grr! Grr! Grr
Grr!   Grr! Grr!
Grr!   Grr!
Grr!   Grr!
Grr!Grr!   Grr!Grr!

If...

dinosaurs were real, then maybe
dragons were as well. And perhaps
one day they'll find a skeleton
beside a craggy cliff, far inside a cave:
a backbone and a tail, a jagged skull,
and those branch-like bones
where the wings would have been.
Or even a whole dragon, perfectly
preserved in Siberian snow:
grey-green and scaly, those two top
canine fangs just jutting over the jaw,
the raging fire of the beast long lost
to the deep sleep of the dead,
those saggy eyelids closed
for ever.

WONDeRFUL

science poems, quiet poems

Night Car Journey

I wake up
sitting in the back seat
not quite sure
if it's real or a dream

and I look up
out through the darkness
out through the silence
to an infinite sky

and the moon bobs
in and out of treetops
turning the world
a ghostly blue

and my eyes
are heavy now
my eyes
are heavy now
my

The Moon Speaks!

I, the moon,
would like it known – I
never follow people home. I
simply do not have the time. And
neither do I ever shine. For what you
often see at night is me reflecting solar
light. And I'm not cheese! No, none of
these: no mozzarellas, cheddars, bries, all
you'll find here – if you please – are my
dusty, empty seas. And cows do not
jump over me. Now that is simply
lunacy! You used to come and
visit me. Oh do return,
I'm lonely, see.

What to Say
If You Meet
A Ghost

Aaa
aaaaaaa
aaaaaaa
!!!   aaaaaa   !!!
!!   aaaaa   !!
!!   aaa   !!
!!   aaaaaaa   !!
aaaaaaaaaaaaa
aaaaaaaaaaaaaaaa
aaaaaaaaaaaaaaaaaaa
aaaaaaaaaaaaaaaaaaaaa
aaaaaaaaaaaaaaaaaaa
aaaaaaaaaaaaaaaa
aaaaaaaaaaaaa
aaaaaaaaa
aaaaaaa
hhhh
hhh
hh
hh
hh
h
!
!
!

The Light

We live
for the light.

Like flowers,
our heads
ever turn
where it's bright.

We yearn when dark
for the planet to spin,
for the light to return
and for life to begin.

Without it,
we wither.
We sleepwalk
through winter.

Moon, tell the sun
to spark out the night.
We need to be loved,
be touched by the light.

The Dark

Why are we so afraid of the dark?
It doesn't bite and it doesn't bark
or chase old ladies round the park
or steal your sweeties for a lark

And though it might not let you see
it lets you have some privacy
and gives you time to go to sleep
provides a place to hide or weep

It cannot help but be around
when beastly things make beastly sounds
when back doors slam and windows creak
when cats have fights and voices shriek

The dark is cosy, still and calm
and never does you any harm
in the loft, below the sink
it's somewhere nice and quiet to think

Deep in cupboards, pockets too
it's always lurking out of view
why won't it come out till it's night?
Perhaps the dark's afraid of light

The Shooting Stars

That night
we went out in the dark
and saw the shooting stars
was one of the best nights ever

It was as if someone
was throwing paint
across the universe

The stars just kept coming
and we 'oohed' and 'aahed'
like on bonfire night

And it didn't matter
they weren't real stars –
just bits of dust on fire
burning up in the atmosphere

And we stayed out there for ages
standing on this tiny planet
staring up at the vast cosmos

And I shivered
with the thrill
of it all

What Stars Are

Stars
are not
the shards of glass
smashed by the gods in anger.

Nor are they
the sparkling souls
of intergalactic travellers.

Not even
the blinking eyes
of invisible skywatchers.

No.

Stars
    are
        stars.

The
dying embers
of ancient fires
that will never know how
they dazzle and delight us
with the final
flickers of their
lives.

The Northern Lights

are not
what
they seem.

Not fireworks
from another realm.

Not portals
into mystic dreams.

Not cosmic curtains, even
swarms of magic dust.

No.

They're simply
solar particles
brought to us
on wild winds
bursting forth
in winter skies
like gifts
to soothe
our tired
eyes.

It's...

The thought or gift that ma**k**es your day.

The hug that says that **i**t's okay.

A**n**d surely it's

what frien**d**s are for.

Right **n**ow

the world ne**e**ds so much more.

It's us human**s** at our best.

In a word it'**s**...

Angelness

You
never
quite know
when you've
met
an
angel.
One may appear at any time at all. It won't have wings.
It won't wear white. Its angelness will
be invisible to the eye. Its human disguise
will be perfect in every way. And there'll be nothing
glamorous: just the quiet,
everyday business of
watching and
waiting
in case
you

fall.

She's...

a zing of yellow,
the fizz in lemonade,
she's the path that keeps me safe,
my shelter and my shade.

She's Springtime's hope.
She's Autumn's gold.
She's Summer's coat
through Winter's cold.

My evening star,
my morning sun,
she's my world and more –
my mum.

Love You More

Do I love you
to the moon and back?
No I love you
more than that

I love you to the desert sands
the mountains, stars
the planets and

I love you to the deepest sea
and deeper still
through history

Before beyond I love you then
I love you now
I'll love you when

The sun's gone out
the moon's gone home
and all the stars are fully grown

When I no longer say these words
I'll give them to the wind, the birds
so that they will still be heard

I
    love
        you

Do You Know What You Are?

A
mammal
with a massive
brain. A mega
mass of **DNA.**
A *biped*
and
a
hominid.
!!   A *primate* and a   !!
!!   *vertebrate.* A *warm-*   !!
!!   *blooded omnivore* with   !!
!!   *carbon molecule*s galore. And   !!
!!   oh yeah, did you know - you are   !!
!!   mostly **H2O**? A *star*-deriving, *time-*   !!
!!   surviving, *earth*-evolving, *space-*   !!
!!   exploring, *future*-seeking,   !!
!!   ever-thinking, speaking,   !!
!!!!   breeding, breathing –   !!!!
b a s i c a l l y   a …
H U M A N
B E I N G
!!   !!
!!   !!
!!   !!
!!   !!
!!   !!
!!   !!
!!!!!!!   !!!!!!!

84

NOW...

The birth of a star.
The beat of a heart.

The arc of an hour.
The bee and the flower.

The flight of a swan.
The weight of the sun.

A river in flood.
The nature of blood.

The future in space
for this human race.

Now that's
what I call
s c i e n c e

This Is Where...

...I learnt to be.
And this is where I learnt to read,
and write and count and act in plays,
and blossom in so many ways...

And this is where I learnt to sing,
express myself, and really think.
And this is where I learnt to dream,
to wonder why and what things mean.

And this is where I learnt to care,
to make good friends, to give, to share,
to kick, to catch, to race, to run.
This is where I had such fun.

And this is where I grew and grew.
And this is where? My primary school.

School Library!

Where are doorways made of words?
That open onto other worlds?
Welcoming all boys and girls?

SCHOOL LIBRARY!

Enter stories wild as dreams.
Meet aliens or fairy queens.
If funky facts are more your scene…

SCHOOL LIBRARY!

Listen, they've got everything,
to make you chuckle, giggle, grin –
be spooked or thrilled. Just come on in.

SCHOOL LIBRARY!

Tempted? Go on, have a look.
You never know, you might get hooked.
Your whole life changed by just one book…

SCHOOL LIBRARY!

That's...

Re **P** etition, rhythm, rhyme,

O r little letters in a line,

a way to s **e** e the world anew,

or much **t** o say in words so few,

so many f **r** uits: a single tree,

a spoken song, that's poetr **y**

!

Where Do You Get Your Ideas From?

From the *space* between my ears
from the *world* behind my eyes
from delving *deep inside* me
where *inspiration* lies

From *memories* that haunt me
from things I *hear* and *see*
from *mystical concoctions*
of *fact* and *fantasy*

From *words* that come and find me
from *dreaming* hard and long
from *life* and *books* and *music*
my *poems*: that's where they're from

How Easily

the present
escapes into the past.
Like raindrops on a lake,

like moths into the dark.
That afternoon you learnt
to swim. The night

you tried to count
the stars. Ever passing
through your hands,

moments disappear
like sand. So catch them.
Trap them. Write them

down. Preserve them
as your memories.
Turn them into

words
      like
            these.

ABOUT THE POET

JAMES CARTER

is an award-winning children's poet, non-fiction writer and musician. An ambassador for National Poetry Day, he travels all over the UK and abroad to give lively, action-packed poetry/music performances, workshops and INSET days. His latest verse non-fiction series for younger readers (Little Tiger Press) is translated into over 8 languages. A former lecturer in Creative Writing/ Children's Literature at Reading University, in the last 19 years James has visited over 1400 Primary/Prep schools in the UK and abroad and has performed at various prestigious festivals including Cheltenham, Hay and Edinburgh. He is the author of CLiPPA-shortlisted collection *Zim Zam Zoom!* (with Nicola Colton). He lives with his family in Oxfordshire.

ABOUT THE ILLUSTRATOR

NEAL LAYTON

is an internationally acclaimed author and illustrator
whose images are prized for their spontaneity and
inventiveness. His picture books include *The Tree,
The Story of Stars, Oscar and Arabella* and *A Planet Full
of Plastic*. Born in Chichester, he was going to be
a scientist but instead studied Graphic Design,
gaining a BA at Newcastle and an MA in Illustration
at Central St Martins. He lives with his family
in Portsmouth, Hampshire.

ALSO BY JAMES CARTER

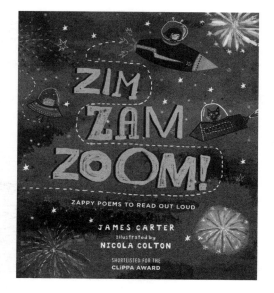

Illustrated by Nicola Colton

*

Shortlisted for the CLiPPA Award

Longlisted for the UKLA Award

"Beautiful book, wonderful words, lovely illustrations"
Poetry Zone

"Great fun to share with a class of children
or as a family at bedtime"
IBBY Link

*